Funniest Bone Animal Jokes

AMUSING Animal JOKES to Tickle Your FUNNY BONE

Amelia LaRoche

Enslow Elementary

an imprint of

Enslow Publishers, Inc.

40 Industrial Road
Box 398
Berkeley Heights, NJ 07922
USA

http://www.enslow.com

For Bob, Walter, and Lou—Always in my heart.

Enslow Elementary, an imprint of Enslow Publishers, Inc.

Enslow Elementary® is a registered trademark of Enslow Publishers, Inc.

Copyright © 2015 by Enslow Publishers, inc.

Library of Congress Cataloging-in-Publication Data
LaRoche, Amelia.
    Amusing animals jokes to tickle your funny bone / Amelia LaRoche.
        pages cm.— (Funniest bone animal jokes)
    Includes index.
    Summary: "Read jokes, limericks, tongue twisters, and knock-knock jokes about a variety of animals.
    Also find out fun and interesting facts about them"—Provided by publisher.
    ISBN 978-0-7660-5968-9
    1. Animals—Juvenile humor. I. Title.
    PN6231.A5L37 2013
    818'.602080362—dc23
                            2013020415

Future editions:
Paperback ISBN: 978-0-7660-5969-6   EPUB ISBN: 978-0-7660-5970-2
Single-User PDF ISBN: 978-0-7660-5971-9   Multi-User PDF ISBN: 978-0-7660-5972-6

Printed in the United States of America

To Our Readers: We have done our best to make sure all Internet addresses in this book were active and appropriate when we went to press. However, the author and the publisher have no control over and assume no liability for the material available on those Internet sites or on other Web sites they may link to. Any comments or suggestions can be sent by e-mail to comments@enslow.com or to the address on the back cover.

Every effort has been made to locate all copyright holders of material used in this book. If any errors or omissions have occurred, corrections will be made in future editions of this book.

Illustration Credits: Clipart.com, pp. 4 (top), 5 (middle, bottom), 11 (middle), 15 (left), 16 (both), 17 (top), 19 (middle, bottom), 22 (middle), 23 (top), 27 (top), 29 (top), 31 (bottom), 33 (all), 34 (middle), 42 (middle); Shutterstock.com: p. 6 (middle); Albert Ziganshin, p. 7 (right); andrewshka, p. 26 (middle); Andrey Makurin, p. 25 (bottom); AntiMartina, p. 44 (bottom left); ayelet-keshet, p. 1 (all); Bannykh Alexey Vladimirovich, pp. 13 (top), 37 (bottom); Basheera Designs, p. 14 (middle left); BlueRingMedia, p. 39 (top); Brian Goff, p. 18 (bottom); cartoons, p. 43 (middle); Christian Baloga, p. 20 (left); Christos Georghiou, p. 41 (top); Dawn Hudson, p. 13 (bottom); dedMazay, pp. 24 (top), 38 (bottom); Deniz Erkorkmaz, p. 21 (top); drewsent, p. 42 (top); Enache Dumitru Bogdan, p. 11 (top); Gorban, pp. 3 (bottom), 21 (bottom), 22 (bottom); Igor Zakowski, p. 35 (bottom); insima, p. 45 (all); IQ Advertising, p. 7 (left); IRINS, p. 18 (middle left); i-zatarn, p. 43 (top); Kathathep, p. 12 (middle); Klara Voskova, pp. 8 (top), 30 (top), 40 (top); Komissar007, p. 22 (top); kostolom3000, p. 6 (bottom); Kseniia Romanova, p. 18 (middle right); kvitka, p. 4 (bottom); JoeyBear, p. 26 (top); Jon Larter, p. 27 (bottom); Laurie Barr, p. 34 (bottom); Linda Bucklin, p. 29 (middle); lineartestpilot, pp. 32 (top), 44 (bottom right); Liusa, p. 36 (top); Lorelyn Medina, p. 25 (top); Luka Skywalker, p. 38 (middle); LYUSHA, p. 19 (top); Maria Bell, p. 38 (top); Matthew Cole, pp. 9 (middle), 39 (middle), 41 (bottom); Memo Angeles, p. 17 (middle); MisterElements, p. 6 (top); mis-Tery, p. 30 (middle left); oculo, p. 3 (middle); Oksana Vasilenko, p. 36 (bottom); Popmarleo, p. 30 (bottom); Pushkin, pp. 28 (top), 35 (top), 39 (bottom); RAStudio, p. 40 (bottom); Rudneu Kiryl, p. 12 (bottom); SahruR, p. 3 (top); Sarawut Padungkwan, pp. 9 (top), 11 (bottom), 14 (top), 15 (top), 20 (right), 34 (top); shockfactor.de, pp. 8 (bottom), 31 (middle); Teguh Mujiono, pp. 12 (top), 25 (middle), 28 (middle); think4photop, p. 18 (top); Thodoris Tibilis, p. 30 (middle right); Tim the Finn, p. 32 (bottom); vichvarupa, p. 41 (middle); VOOK, p. 9 (bottom); wizdata1, p. 44 (top); Yayayoyo, p. 36 (middle); © Thinkstock: © alena drozd/iStock, p. 13 (middle); © BiterBig/iStock, p. 29 (bottom); © Claudia Lema/iStock, p. 37 (middle); © dedMazay/iStock, p. 10 (top), 14 (middle right); © Dennis Cox/Hemera, p. 5 (top); Dorling Kindersley, p. 37 (top); © Irina Makhova/Hemera, p. 28 (bottom); © Liudmila Pantelejenkova/iStock, p. 17 (bottom); © -M-I-S-H-A-/iStock, p. 2; Norman Young, p. 10 (bottom); © Oleksiy Tsuper/iStock, p. 43 (bottom); © Pavel Bortel/Hemera, p. 23 (bottom); © Thodoris_Tibilis/iStock, p. 40 (middle); © vectorcartoons/iStock, p. 24 (bottom).

Cover Illustrations: Shutterstock.com: Gorban (front); Teguh Mujiono (back).

Contents

Being Silly Fur Silly's Sake

Why did the hamster stop running on his wheel?

It wasn't getting him anywhere.

What does a mink wear?

A mink coat, of course!

The skunk skulked.

What did the fox say when the farmer shined a light in the henhouse?

"Cluck, cluck!"

WHAT IS A KNOCK-KNOCK JOKE?

A knock-knock joke starts with a knock at a pretend door by someone whose first name makes sense, but whose last name is a laugh.

DID YOU KNOW?

Did you know that a group of foxes is called a skulk? It's true! Other weird names for groups of animals include murder for crows, cackle for hyenas, pride for lions, and lounge for lizards.

What do skunks do with catalogs?

Odor from them.

Knock, knock.

Who's there?

Bunny.

Bunny who?

Bunny you should ask!

A flurry of fleece flew from the sheep.

FUN FACT

A rabbit named Herman who lives in Germany weighs twenty-two pounds and measures a little over three feet. He can eat a bale of hay every week! Herman is a German giant, which is a type of domestic rabbit.

Knock, knock.

Who's there?

Foxy.

Foxy who?

Foxy broken doorbell—I'm tired of knocking.

What's invisible and smells like carrots?

Rabbit breath.

Limerick

Said the fox who was kept in a cage,
"I hear that fur coats are the rage,
But it doesn't seem fair
To take my red hair—
I'd rather wear it myself as I age."

When choosing to live with rabbits
Remember they have toothy habits.
They chew, chew, chew,
And they're still not through,
Which is why they need lots of carrots.

What looks like half a guinea pig?

The other half of the guinea pig.

Why are rabbits so lucky?

They have four rabbit's feet.

Why do rabbits have such big ears?

So they can hare you coming.

WHAT IS A LIMERICK?

A limerick is a funny five-line poem. Lines one, two, and five are longer and they rhyme. Lines three and four are shorter and they rhyme.

2 Hooves and Horns

What did the vet say to the pony who came to him with a sore throat?

"You're just a little hoarse."

Knock, knock.

Who's there?

Moo.

Moo who?

What are you—a cow or an owl?

Why did the deer have to get braces?

He had buck teeth.

What's black and white and red all over?

A zebra with a sunburn.

Horses have hard hooves.

FUN FACT

Did you know that one meaning of the word *dactyl* is "toe"? It's true! Hoofed animals with an even number of toes are called artiodactyls (ar tee oh DAK tuls). These include pigs and goats, who have two toes on each foot. Animals with an odd number of toes—like horses, who have one hoof on each foot, and rhinoceroses, who have three toes on each foot—are called perissodactyls (puh RIS uh dak tuls). Try saying that without putting your hoof in your mouth! (By the way, more than one hoof gives you hooves. An animal with hooves is hoofed. HOOF! What a word!)

What do you get when you cross a giraffe with a book?

A long story.

Want to hear a dirty joke?

A white horse fell in the mud.

Why did the gnu cross the busy road?

Because he didn't gnu any better.

A mammal with hooves is an ungulate.
They're described that way in the science lit.
They can have several toes
But when quizzed, who knows?
Can they count them or will they bungle it?

Why did the cow
cross the road?

To get to the
udder side.

Limerick

Rhinoceroses have been known to charge
When they hear something loud or scary or large.
They run at the sound
But can also be found
At department stores charging on credit cards.

FUN FACT

Rhinos can reach speeds of thirty-five miles per hour! Despite how fast and fearsome these horned beasts seem, rhinos are vegetarians that eat leaves, thorny bushes, fruit, and grass. They have terrible eyesight but sharp hearing. They are excellent parents—baby rhinos stay with their mothers for three years. Rhinos can live to be forty years old.

Shell Games

How do snails text each other?

On their shell phones.

Can a clan of clams clip coupons?

Why are snails so strong?

They carry their houses on their backs.

DID YOU KNOW?

Did you know that there is a type of snail called a nudibranch (NOO dih brahnk) that doesn't have a shell? It's true! "Nudibranch" means "naked gill," and some of these sea creatures come in stunning, bright colors. Since they don't have shells to protect them, the colors might be a way to warn hungry predators: "Don't eat me—I taste terrible!"

Why did the mollusk get kicked out of the school play?

Because when he had to say his lines, he clammed up.

Why do squids swim in the ocean?

Because swimming on land is too hard.

What do snails do for a living?

They polish snails at snail salons.

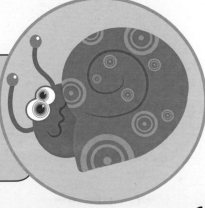

Limerick

There once was a snail called Kelly
Who had a very hard shelly.
She was safe in her home
In the waves' foamy foam,
But inside it, she jiggled like jelly.

FUN FACT

There are more than 50,000 known species of mollusks. Among them are snails, clams, mussels, squids, and octopuses. Most mollusks have three body parts: a head, a body, and a "foot." Some mollusks have long arms or tentacles. Some mollusks have shells but not all of them.

Shelley sells seashells by the seashore.

Why are oysters so wise?

They always have pearls of wisdom.

Limerick

Lydia was a lovely squid
Who lived in a fish tank with Sid.
The two were friends
But they met sad ends
In a boiling pot with a lid.

WHAT IS A TONGUE TWISTER?

It's a saying that makes you trip over your tongue, so watch your step while you're saying one!

Fun With Fins

Why are fish so smart?

They live in schools.

What kind of fish come out at night?

Starfish.

Knock, knock.

Who's there?

Tuna.

Tuna who?

Tuna piano for ya?

DID YOU KNOW?

Did you know that fish are smarter than they might seem? It's true! According to researchers, fish of several species that have been caught on a hook learn from the painful experience and try to avoid repeating it.

Why did the fish cross the road?

To get to the other tide.

What do you call fish with no eyes?

F sh.

What do fish hate seeing in their flowerbeds?

Seaweeds.

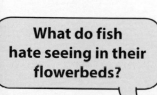

What do sharks eat with peanut butter?

Jellyfish.

Sam the Shark's nickname is "Vicious"
Since his favorite fresh food is fishes.
But that name is unfair,
Sam is quick to declare,
Since all sharks think fish are delicious!

Knock, knock.

Who's there?

Flounder.

Flounder who?

Flounder key. Can I let myself in?

The jellyfish floated in a fissure.

There once was a goldfish named Han
Who was turning into a crank.
He swam day and night,
But try as he might,
He couldn't get out of his tank.

FUN FACT

Fish have been swimming the seas for more than 450 million years. Scientists believe they were here even before dinosaurs began roaming the earth.

Why is it so easy to weigh a fish?

Because it comes with its own scales.

What do you get when you cross a fish and an elephant?

Swimming trunks.

Sleek sharks swim swiftly.

5 Extinction Junction

Which type of dinosaur could jump higher than a four-story building?

What do you call a nearsighted dinosaur?

An I-don't-think-he-saurus.

All of them. Four-story buildings can't jump.

Limerick

The smartest dinosaur, the Troodon,
Had a big brain and hands that could grasp on
But if it was so smart,
Then tell me this part:
Exactly where have all the Troodons gone?

DID YOU KNOW?

Did you know that one of the heaviest dinosaurs was Brachiosaurus? It's true. Just one Brachiosaurus weighed as much as seventeen African elephants.

What do you get when you let dinosaurs drive?

Tyrannosaurus wrecks.

What's the hardest kind of dinosaur to ride?

A bronco-saurus.

FUN FACT

Dinosaurs lived hundreds of millions of years ago and came in an amazing range of shapes and sizes. One that we are just learning about is the tiny *Pegomastax africanus* ("thick jaw from Africa"). It was no bigger than a house cat. This nimble, two-legged dinosaur had porcupine-like quills and a beak with fangs that it used to eat plants.

Why are dinosaurs extinct?

I don't know—and there aren't any left to ask.

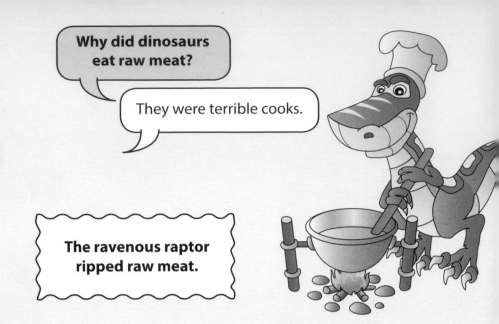

Why did dinosaurs eat raw meat?

They were terrible cooks.

The ravenous raptor ripped raw meat.

Limerick

The Dromiceiomimus could run very fast.
In every race run, it never came in last.
The reason is clear,
It was running in fear
Of trying to say its own name, which is vast.

Knock, knock.

Who's there?

Terry.

Terry who?

Terry-dactyl, and if you open the door, I'm going to eat you.

6 Bungle in the Jungle

What kind of key opens bananas?

A monkey.

Why don't monkeys play games in the jungle?

There are too many cheetahs.

DID YOU KNOW?

Did you know that monkeys are divided into two groups? It's true! Old World monkeys live in Africa and Asia. A mandrill is an Old World monkey. New World monkeys live in South America. A spider monkey is a New World monkey.

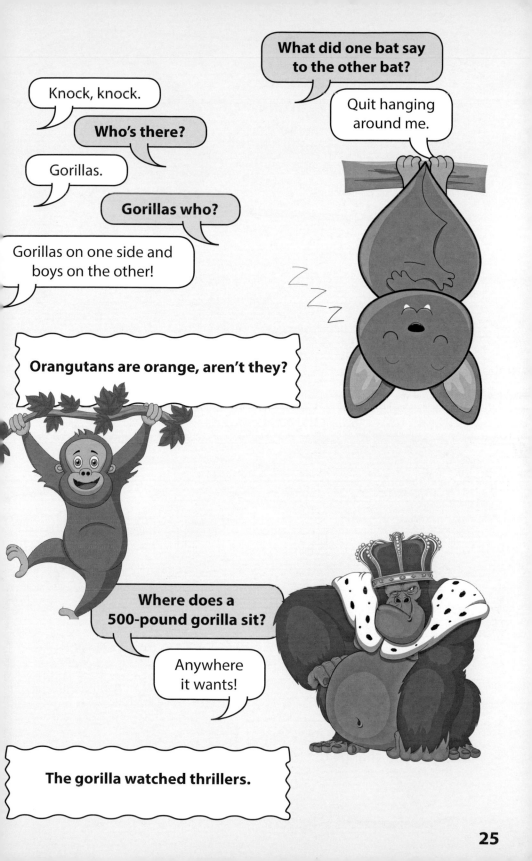

FUN FACT

Apes don't have tails and they aren't monkeys. Gorillas, orangutans, chimpanzees, and bonobos are all apes. Orangutans are the world's largest tree-dwelling animals.

Limerick

There once was a sleek black jaguar,
Who lived in a forest afar.
She climbed up tall trees,
Ran fast as the breeze,
And gave her name to a speedy sports car.

Knock, knock.

Who's there?

Monkey.

Monkey who?

Monkey won't work! Did you change the lock?

Where do tigers work out?

The jungle gym.

There once was a great ape named Stan
Who decided to get a spray tan.
It turned him bright red
From his toes to his head—
What a goofy orangutan!

What time is it when an elephant sits on your watch?

It's time to get a new watch. And if you were wearing the watch at that moment, it might be time to get a new arm.

What happens when a boat sinks in a river full of piranhas?

It gets a skeleton crew.

hat's gigantic and bright blue?

An elephant holding his breath.

27

7 Tickled to Death by Feathers

What do you get when you cross a parrot with a shark?

A bird that will talk your ear off.

Knock, knock.

Who's there?

Owl.

Owl who?

Yup, that's what an owl does.

DID YOU KNOW?

Did you know that crows are among the smartest birds in the world? It's true! One of the many clever things these birds do is drop hard nuts on roads so that cars will run over them and crack the shells.

What kind of bird is always out of breath?

A puffin.

What's the most popular bird at dinnertime?

A swallow.

I live with a parrot named Penny,
Whose skills and charms are many.
She can speak several words;
She can fly with the birds;
And she lays eggs as well as a henny.

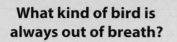

What do you call a seagull flying over a bay?

A bagel.

How did the hen bake her cakes?

From scratch.

Why did the fool buy birdseed?

So he could plant it and grow birds.

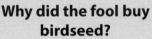
Limerick

There once was a canary yellow
Who was a courageous fellow.
He simply could not sing,
But instead of quitting,
He taught himself how to bellow.

Our fine, feathered friends fly freely.

FUN FACT

A budgie named Puck was accepted into *The Guinness Book of World Records* as the bird with the largest vocabulary. The little parakeet could say 1,728 words!

The sleek swan swam on the pond.

Knock, knock.

Who's there?

Chicken.

Chicken who?

Chicken in to see how you are!

The crow cawed and croaked.

What kind of bird can carry heavy loads?

A crane.

Knock, knock.

Who's there?

Lion.

Lion who?

Lion down on the job again?

What happens when it rains cats and dogs?

People step in poodles.

When are black cats bad luck?

When you're a canary.

DID YOU KNOW?

Did you know that a cat's collarbones aren't connected to its other bones? It's true! The collarbones are buried in its shoulder muscles, which means a cat can squeeze through any opening that's only as big as its head.

Why didn't the fool who lost his dog put an ad in the newspaper?

Because he figured his dog wouldn't be able to read it.

What do you get when you cross a tiger with a housecat?

New furniture.

What is a puppy after it's ten days old?

Eleven days old.

Why don't cats eat lemons?

They don't want to be sour pusses.

How do fleas get around?

They take the greyhound.

The cranky cat caused a commotion.

Limerick

Canines are dogs and felines are cats.
The difference is clear—it lies in the pats.
Dogs beg to be stroked,
But cats feel provoked
Unless they thought of it first, and that's that.

FUN FACT

A long time ago, wolves became domesticated, leading to today's dogs. Scientists can't pinpoint when it happened, but it was at least 12,000 years ago, and maybe as long as 35,000 years ago. It's hard to believe Chihuahuas, poodles, and bulldogs are related to wolves, but they are all "canids." Other canids include jackals, hyenas, coyotes, and foxes.

Limerick

The male lion is a majestic beast
That tips the scales at 300 pounds, at least.
But when it's time to hunt
It's the females that grunt—
They're more skillful than males at catching a feast.

The dotted Dalmatian drooled.

Knock, knock.

Who's there?

Bee.

Bee who?

Beware of dog!

What did the buffalo say to his son when he left for school?

"Bison!"

Why did the fool oil her mouse?

To fix the squeak.

What's a penguin's favorite food?

Iceberg lettuce.

DID YOU KNOW?

Did you know that snakes have between two hundred and four hundred bones in their spines? It's true! Humans have only thirty-three spine bones. Snakes could tell us to get a backbone!

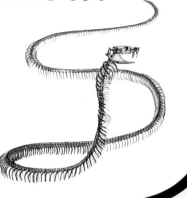

Knock, knock.

Who's there?

Cow.

Cow who?

Cowculator's broken, so nothing adds up!

Big backbones make for bravado.

Why do whales live in salt water?

Because pepper water would make them sneeze.

What did the vet rub on the sick pig?

Oink-ment.

Voles, moles, and bulls share bones, blood, and fur.

Knock, knock.

Who's there?

Whale.

Whale who?

Whale, are you going to let me in or not?

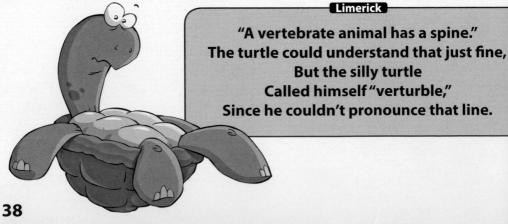

Limerick

"A vertebrate animal has a spine."
The turtle could understand that just fine,
But the silly turtle
Called himself "verturble,"
Since he couldn't pronounce that line.

FUN FACT

Vertebrates are animals with backbones, also called spines. If you're holding this book, the chances are excellent that you are a vertebrate. Mammals and fish are vertebrates. Birds and reptiles are vertebrates, too. Turtles have backbones that are attached to the inside of their shells. Invertebrates are animals that don't have backbones, such as snails, spiders, and octopuses.

Limerick

There once was a snake named Jess
Who used to lie motionless.
But Jess was no fool:
He went to snake school,
Where he learned how to move like an "S."

How do porcupines kiss?

Carefully!

Why are snakes hard to fool?

They have no legs to pull.

39

Swamp Things

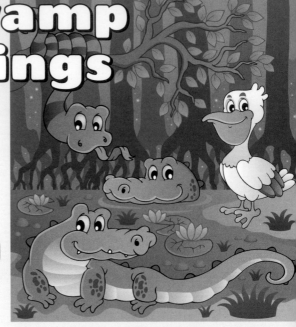

What do you call an alligator in a vest?

An investigator.

What did the beaver say to the tree?

"It's been nice gnawing ya!"

The firefly flashed a message.

Knock, knock.

Who's there?

Otter.

Otter who?

Otter let me in—
I brought dinner!

What did the salamander say when he asked for directions?

"I'm newt here."

Why was the snake so quiet?

She had a frog in her throat.

DID YOU KNOW?

Did you know that beavers slap their long, flat tails on the surface of the water when they sense danger? It's true! The sound sends a warning to other beavers in the area. These strong swimmers can stay underwater for up to fifteen minutes.

What did one toad say to the other toad?

"Wart's new?"

What happened to the frog that broke down?

He got toad.

Knock, knock.

Who's there?

Tad.

Tad who?

Tadpole! What? You were expecting a frog?

What animal has the most lives?

A frog, because he croaks every day!

What did the taxi driver say to the frog?

"Hop in."

Limerick

There once was a beaver named Keith
Who was proud of his store-bought teeth.
They looked very bold—
They were made of gold
With hydraulics built in underneath.

FUN FACT

After a female Darwin's frog lays her eggs, the male guards them for two weeks, until they hatch. Then he carries the tadpoles in his vocal pouch until they develop into tiny frogs that hop out of his mouth and swim away!

"No regrets" is the egret's secret.

What do you get when you cross a frog with a bunny?

A ribbit!

Limerick

Moose often hang around ponds,
Grazing on hard-to-reach fronds.
But given a choice,
They'd probably rejoice
If greens came from magic wands.

Make an Animal Book

Here's What You Will Need:

- paper
- colored markers
- glue stick
- scissors
- stapler

Directions:

1. Find pictures in old magazines or online of animals that interest you.

2. Cut out or print the pictures.

3. Use the glue stick to attach each picture to a larger piece of paper.

4. Look up information about each animal and write it under the picture. Try to find interesting and unusual facts!

5. Draw a cover for your book.

6. Staple all the pages together.

Words to Know

bravado—Boldness.

bungle—To do something in a clumsy way; also, something that was done poorly.

commotion—Noisy confusion.

domestic—Tame.

domesticated—Trained to live with humans.

extinct—No longer in existence.

fissure—A narrow opening in rock or earth.

frond—A large leaf, especially one that has many divisions.

hydraulics—A system of moving objects by pushing liquids through pipes.

joke—Something that is said to make people laugh.

junction—A place where things come together.

mammal—Any of a group of animals that have a backbone, fur or hair, and warm blood, and whose mothers produce milk for their young.

predator—A hunter.

skulk—To move in a sneaky way; also, a group of foxes.

tentacle—A long flexible body part that is used for feeding or grasping.

ungulate—An animal with hooves.

vegetarian—A plant eater.

vocabulary—A collection of words that are used regularly.

Read More

Books

Dahl, Michael, Kathi Wagner, Aubrey Wagner, and Aileen Weintraub. *The Everything Kids' Giant Book of Jokes, Riddles & Brain Teasers*. Avon, Mass.: F + W Media, 2010.

Elliot, Rob. *Zoolarious Animal Jokes for Kids*. Grand Rapids, Mich.: Revell, 2012.

Phillips, Bob. *Super Incredible Knock-Knock Jokes for Kids*. Eugene, Oreg.: Harvest House Publishers, 2007.

Internet Addresses

Ducksters: Kid Jokes
http://www.ducksters.com/jokesforkids/animals.php

Jokes 'N Jokes: Kids Jokes
http://www.jokesnjokes.net/funny.jokes.amusing.humor.laughs/kids.htm

National Institute of Environmental Health Sciences: Kids' Pages: Jokes Galore!
http://kids.niehs.nih.gov/games/jokes/jokes_galore.htm

Index

A
alligators, 40
apes, 26, 27

B
bats, 25
beavers, 40, 41, 42
birds, 28–31, 39
bison/buffalo, 36
budgie, 31
bulls, 38
bunnies, 5, 43

C
canaries, 30, 32
canids, 35
cats, 21, 32–35
clams, 12, 14
cows, 8, 11, 37
crows, 5, 28, 31

D
deer, 8
dinosaurs, 19, 20–23
dogs, 32–35

E
earth, 19
egrets, 43
elephants, 19, 20, 27

F
fireflies, 40
fish, 16–19, 39
fleas, 34
foxes, 4, 6, 35
frogs, 41, 42, 43

G
German giant, 6
giraffes, 9
gnus, 9, 10
goats, 9, 10
gorillas, 25, 26
guinea pigs, 7
*The Guinness Book of
   World Records,* 31

H
hamsters, 4
hares, 7
Herman, 6
horses, 8, 9, 10
hyenas, 5, 35

I
invertebrates, 39

J
jellyfish, 17, 18

L
lions, 5, 32, 35
lizards, 5

M
mammals, 11, 39
mice, 36
mink, 4
mollusks, 13, 14
monkeys, 24, 26
moose, 43

N
nudibranch, 12

O

octopuses, 14, 39
orangutans, 25, 26, 27
otters, 41
owls, 8, 28

P
pigs, 9, 38
porcupines, 15, 21, 39
predators, 12
Puck, 31

R
rabbits, 6, 7
rhinoceroses, 9, 11

S
salamanders, 41
scientists, 19, 35
sharks, 17, 18, 19, 28
skunks, 4, 5
snails, 12, 13, 14, 15, 39
snakes, 37, 39, 41
squids, 13, 14, 15

T
tigers, 26, 33
toads, 42
turtles, 38, 39

V
vertebrates, 36–39

W
whales, 37, 38

Z
zebras, 8